SQL Server 2017

A Practical Guide for Beginners

Table of Contents

Introduction

A database management system helps us to create and maintain our data. SQL Server is a database management system with highly productive features. This makes it a good database management system for use in a production environment. It allows you to use it via the SQL Server Management Studio, which is good for beginners as it provides a graphical user environment or through the Transact-SQL, which is good for experienced users and those with good computer programming knowledge. This book guides you on how to use SQL Server 2017, which is the latest release of SQL Version. It guides you on how to perform the various operations using both the SQL Server Management Studio and the Transact-SQL. Enjoy reading!

Chapter 1- Installing Microsoft SQL Server 2017

The installation of SQL Server can be done through the Installation Wizard, the command prompt, or through simper. However, before you can install the SQL Server on your system, it is good for you to check and ensure that your system meets all the requirements.

After that, download the version of SQL Server 2017 that you need to install. This can be the Express edition, the Developer edition, or the Evaluation edition.

Installation on Server Core

SQL Server can be installed on the Core Server installation. We will be guiding you on how to install the SQL 2017 on the Server Core. With this type of installation, you will be provided with a minimal environment in which you will be able to run a number of server roles. With this, the requirements and management roles will be reduced as well as the attack surface for the server roles.

Prerequisites

1. .NET Framework 4.6.1- this is required for you to install any version of SQL Server 2017 except the Express edition. If this is not installed, then the SQL Server setup will install it automatically. A reboot will be required, but if you need to avoid this, make sure that you have installed .NET Framework before you can run the SQL Server setup.
2. Windows Installer 4.5- this comes with the Server Core installation.

3. Windows PowerShell- this comes with the Server Core installation.

4. Java Runtime- this will be required for you to install and use the Polybase.

If you are using SQL Server 2014, it is also possible for you to upgrade.

When installing the SQL Server 2017 on the Server Core, you will not be allowed to do it via the installation wizard. The installation of this in Server Core is supported in full quiet mode by use of the /Q parameter, or the Quiet Simple mode by use of the /QS parameter.

If you need to install only some features, you should use the /FEATURES parameter and then specify the feature values or the parent feature. Here are the feature parameters which can be used:

1. SQLENGINE- this will install only the Database Engine.

2. REPLICATION- this will install the Replication Engine together with the Database Engine.

3. FULLTEXT- this will install the FULLTEXT component together with the Database Engine.
4. AS- this will install the Analysis Services components.

5. IS- this will install the Integration Services components.

6. CONN- this will install the connectivity components.

7. ADVANCEDANALYTICS- this will install the R services, and the Database Engine will be required.

The Installation Options

The following are some of the options which can be used for installation of SQL Server 2017 on the Server Core operating system:

1. Using the command line

If you need to install specific features from the command line, you should use the /FEATURES parameter. You should then specify the parent feature of feature values. Here is an example:

Setup.exe /qs /ACTION=Install /FEATURES=SQLEngine,Replication /INSTANCENAME=MSSQLSERVER /SQLSVCACCOUNT="\<DomainName\UserName> " /SQLSVCPASSWORD="\<StrongPassword>" /SQLSYSADMINACCOUNTS="\<DomainName\UserName>" /AGTSVCACCOUNT="NT AUTHORITY\Network Service" /TCPENABLED=1 /IACCEPTSQLSERVERLICENSETERMS

2. Installing using the Configuration File

The configuration file can only be used from the command line. The file has a basic structure of the parameter as well as a descriptive comment. The configuration file you specify on the command prompt should have an .INI extension in its name. The example given below can be used for installation of an instance of SQL Server featuring the Database Engine:

` ` `

**; SQL Server Configuration File
[OPTIONS]**

; Specifies the Setup work flow, such as INSTALL, UNINSTALL, or UPGRADE. This parameter is required.

ACTION="Install"

; Specifies features to be installed, uninstalled, or upgraded. The features include SQLEngine, Replication, AS, IS, FullText, and Conn.

8

```
FEATURES=SQLENGINE

; Specify a default or a named instance.
MSSQLSERVER forms the default instance for the
non-Express editions and the SQLExpress for the
Express editions. This parameter is needed when
installing ssNoVersion Database Engine, and the
Analysis Services (AS).

INSTANCENAME="MSSQLSERVER"

; Specify the Instance ID for the ssNoVersion
features you have specified. ssNoVersion
directory structure, registry structure, and service
names will incorporate the instance ID of the
ssNoVersion instance.

INSTANCEID="MSSQLSERVER"

; Account for ssNoVersion service: Domain\User
or system account.

SQLSVCACCOUNT="NT Service\MSSQLSERVER"

; Windows account(s) to provision as ssNoVersion
system administrators.

SQLSYSADMINACCOUNTS="\<DomainName\Us
erName>"

; Accept the License agreement to continue with
Installation

IAcceptSQLServerLicenseTerms="True"

    ```
```

The connectivity components can be installed by use of the
following example:
```

```
; SQL Server Configuration File
[OPTIONS]

; Specifies a Setup work flow, like INSTALL,
UNINSTALL, or UPGRADE. This is a required
parameter.

ACTION="Install"

; Specifies features to install, uninstall, or upgrade.
The lists of features include SQLEngine, FullText,
Replication, AS, IS, and Conn.

FEATURES=Conn

; Specifies acceptance of License Terms

IAcceptSQLServerLicenseTerms="True
```

We can then install all the supported features in the Server Core:

```
; SQL Server Configuration File
[OPTIONS]
; Specifies a Setup work flow, like INSTALL,
UNINSTALL, or UPGRADE. This is a required
parameter.

ACTION="Install"

; Specifies features to be installed, uninstalled, or
upgraded. The lists of the features include
SQLEngine, Replication, AS, FullText, IS, and Conn.

FEATURES=SQLENGINE,FullText,Replication,AS,IS,
Conn
```

; Specify the default or a named instance. MSSQLSERVER forms the default instance for the non-Express editions and the SQLExpress for the Express editions. The parameter is needed when installing ssNoVersion Database Engine (SQL), or the Analysis Services (AS).

INSTANCENAME="MSSQLSERVER"

; Specify the Instance ID for ssNoVersion features which you have specified. The ssNoVersion directory structure, registry structure, and the service names will incorporate instance ID of ssNoVersion instance.

INSTANCEID="MSSQLSERVER"

; Account for ssNoVersion service: Domain\User or system account.

SQLSVCACCOUNT="NT Service\MSSQLSERVER"

; Windows account(s) to provision as ssNoVersion system administrators.

SQLSYSADMINACCOUNTS="\<DomainName\UserN ame>"

; The name of account which the Analysis Services service runs under.
ASSVCACCOUNT= "NT Service\MSSQLServerOLAPService"

; Specifics the list of the administrator accounts which need to be provisioned.

ASSYSADMINACCOUNTS="\<DomainName\UserNa me>"

; Specifies server mode of Analysis Services instance. Valid values are MULTIDIMENSIONAL, POWERPIVOT or TABULAR. ASSERVERMODE is case-sensitive. All values must be written in upper case.

ASSERVERMODE="MULTIDIMENSIONAL"

; Optional value, specifying the state of TCP protocol for ssNoVersion service. Supported values include: 0 to disable the TCP protocol, and 1 to enable the TCP protocol.

TCPENABLED=1

;Specifies acceptance of License Terms

IAcceptSQLServerLicenseTerms="True"

You can launch the setup by use of the configuration file. The configuration file can be specified on the command line as shown below:

Setup.exe /QS /ConfigurationFile=MyConfigurationFile.INI

If you need to specify the password on the command line rather than in the configuration file, do it as follows:

Setup.exe /QS /SQLSVCPASSWORD="************" /ASSVCPASSWORD="************" /ConfigurationFile=MyConfigurationFile.INI

Configuring Remote Access

It is also possible for you to configure remote access to the SQL Server 2017 instance readily running on Server Core. This will be done by use of SQLCMD.exe locally then run the following statements against the instance of Server Core:

EXEC sys.sp_configure N'remote access', N'1'

GO

RECONFIGURE WITH OVERRIDE

GO

SQL Server Browser Service

The default setting is that the browser service comes disabled. If the SQL server instance running on the Server Core has this disabled, open the command prompt then run the following command:

sc config SQLBROWSER start= auto

After that, run the following command so as to start the service:

net start SQLBROWSER

Enabling TCP/IP

For you to enable the TCP/IP protocol on the SQL Server running on Server Core, we use the Windows PowerShell. The following steps can help in this:

1. Our assumption is that you are doing it on a computer which is running the Windows Server 2008 R2 Server Core SP1. Launch the Task Manager.

2. Click "New Task" from the "Applications" tab.

3. In the dialog box for "Create New Task", type in "sqlps.exe" in its open field then click on "OK". The Microsoft SQL Server window will be opened.

4. You can then run the script given below in this window for the TCP/IP protocol to be enabled:

```
$smo = 'Microsoft.SqlServer.Management.Smo.'
$wmi = new-object ($smo +
'Wmi.ManagedComputer')
# Enable the TCP protocol on the default instance.  If
the instance is named, replace MSSQLSERVER with
the instance name in the following line.

$uri = "ManagedComputer[@Name='" + (get-item
env:\computername).Value +
"']/ServerInstance[@Name='MSSQLSERVER']/Serve
rProtocol[@Name='Tcp']"
$Tcp = $wmi.GetSmoObject($uri)
$Tcp.IsEnabled = $true
$Tcp.Alter()
$Tcp
```

Sometimes, you may close the command prompt accidentally and need to open a new one. The following steps can help you achieve this:

1. Press Ctrl+Shift+Esc so as to display the Task Manager.

2. On the "Applications" tab, click on "New Task."

3. In the dialog box for "Create New Task," type "cmd" in its "Open" field and then click "OK."

Installation from the Installation Wizard

You can install the SQL Server 2017 from the SQL Server setup installation wizard. The feature comes with a single feature tree which can be used for installation of all the SQL Server components. The installation can be done by following the steps given below:

1. Insert the media with the SQL Server. Double click Setup.exe from the root folder. If you need to install from the network share, just identify the folder on the share and then click on Setup.exe.
2. The Installation wizard will run the SQL Server Installation Center. To install an instance of this, move to the left navigation wizard and then click on "Installation." Click the "New SQL Server stand-alone installation or add features to an existing installation."

3. Choose whether you want to install a free version of SQL Server or a production version with a product key. Click on "Next" to continue.

4. Review the license agreements and then accept. Click 'Next."

5. On the Setup Role page, choose "SQL Server Feature Installation," and then click on "Next" so as to continue.

6. On the Feature Selection Page, choose the components which you need to be installed.

7. On the Instance Configuration page, choose whether to install a named instance or a default instance.

8. In the Server Configuration-Service Accounts page, choose whether you need to specify the login accounts for the SQL Server services. This will be determined by the features which you chose for installation. All the SQL Server services can be assigned to one login account. You may also specify the services to be started automatically, manually, or even disable them.

9. On the "Database Engine Configuration - Server Configuration" page, specify the following details:

Security Mode- chooses whether to use the Windows Authentication mode or the Mixed Authentication Mode for your SQL Server instance.

If you select the Mixed Mode authentication, then you will have to type in a strong password for the administrator. SQL Server Administrators- you should specify one or more system administrators for the instance of SQL Server. To add some new account for the running SQL Server setup, click on "Add Current User." If you need to add or remove an account from the list of the system administrators, click on Add or Remove and then edit users, group lists, or the computers to be granted administrative privileges for the SQL Server instances.

For you to specify the non-default installation directories, use the Database Engine Configuration. If you need to install to the default directories, just click on "Next."

10. Use the page for "Analysis Services Configuration — Account Provisioning" for specification of the server mode and accounts or users which will have the administrator permissions for the Analysis Services. The Server mode specifies the memory and storage subsystems which will be used on the server.

11. Use the page for "Distributed Replay Controller Configuration" so as to grant administrative privileges to the users whom you need to access the Distributed Replay controller service. This will give them unlimited access to the service. Click the button named "Add Current User" so as to be able to add users whom you need to grant access to Distributed Replay controller service. Click on the "Add" button so as to add the permissions to the service. If you need to remove permissions from the service, click on the "Remove" button. Click "Next" so as to continue.

12. The page for Distributed Replay Client Configuration can be used for specifying the users to be granted access

permissions to the Distributed Replay Client service. These users will then have an unlimited access to the Distributed Replay Client service. The "Controller Name" parameter is optional with a default value of <blank>. Type in the name for the controller which the client computer will be communicating with for Distributed Replay Client service.

13. On the Ready to install page, click on "Install" so as to continue with the installation process. The installation process will show you the progress and once complete, a "Close" button will be appear. Click on this button. In case you are prompted to restart the computer, just do it.

Chapter 2- Surface Area Configuration

After a new installation of SQL Server, the default setting is that the majority of the features are disabled. The SQL Server starts only a number of features so that it can reduce the number of features which can be attacked by a potential attacker. The system administrator can control this during installation or even after installation by enabling and disabling the services.

Protocols, Connection, and Startup Options

The SQL Server Configuration Manager should be used for starting and stopping services, configuring the startup options, and enabling the protocols, as well as the other configuration options. The following steps will help you launch the SQL Server Configuration Manager:

1. Click on Start, then All Programs, and then Microsoft SQL Server 2017. Click on Configuration Tools, and then SQL Server Configuration Manager.

   Use the area for SQL Server Services so as to start the components and then configure automatic starting options.

2. Use the area for SQL Server Network Configuration so as to enable the connection protocols and the connection options such as the fixed TCP/IP ports and forcing encryption.

Enabling and Disabling Features

The process of enabling and disabling the SQL Server features can be done in the facets of the SQL Server Management Studio. The following steps can help you configure the surface area by use of the facets:

1. Connect to the SQL Server component from the Management Studio.

2. Right click on the server and then click on Facets from the Object Explorer.

3. In the dialog box for View Facets, expand the Facet list, and then choose the necessary Surface Area Configuration facet. This can be the Surface Area Configuration, **the** Surface Area Configuration for Analysis Services, **or the** Surface Area Configuration for Reporting Services.

4. In the area for Facet Properties, choose the values which you need for every property. Click OK.

If you need to check the configuration of a facet on a periodical basis, just use the Policy-Based Management.

Chapter 3- Creating a Database

In this chapter, you will learn how to create a new database in SQL Server 2017 by use of either Transact-SQL or SQL Server Management Studio. Note that the maximum number of databases which can be created in an instance of Microsoft SQL Server is 32,767. The CREATE DATABASE statement can only be executed in the autocommit mode, and it is not supported in an implicit or even explicit transaction.

Creating a Database in SQL Server Management Studio

The following steps will help you create a new database:

1. Open the Object Explorer, then establish a connection to the SQL Server Database Engine instance, and then expand the instance.

2. Right-click on Databases and then click on New Database.

3. Type in the name for the new database.

4. If you need to accept the default settings for the database, just click on "OK," otherwise, just continue with the steps given below.

5. To change the name of the owner, just click on the ellipsis (...) so as to change the owner.

6. If you need to change the default values for the primary data as well as the transaction log files, just move to the Database files grid, then click on the appropriate cell, and type its new value.

7. If you need to change the database collation, choose the "Options" page and then select a collation from the provided list.

8. If you need to change the recovery model for the database, open the "Options" page and then choose one of the recovery models from the list.

9. To change the database options, open the Options page and then change the options for the database.

10. If you need to add a new filegroup, click on the Filegroups page. Click on Add and then type in the values for the new filegroup.

11. If you need to add an extended property to the database, choose the page for Extended Properties. In the column for Name, enter the name for the extended property. In the column for Value, enter the text for the extended property. A good example is a statement or statements describing the database.

12. Click "OK" so as to create the database.

Using Transact-SQL

The following steps will help you create a database by use of Transact-SQL:

1. Establish a connection to the database engine.

2. On the standard bar, click on New Query.

3. In the query window, paste the example given below and then click on Execute.

   USE master ;
   GO
   CREATE DATABASE Class
   ON
   (NAME = Class_dat,

```
     FILENAME = 'C:\Program Files\Microsoft
SQL
Server\MSSQL13.MSSQLSERVER\MSSQL\DAT
A\classdat.mdf',

     SIZE = 10,
     MAXSIZE = 50,
     FILEGROWTH = 5 )
LOG ON
( NAME = Class_log,
     FILENAME = 'C:\Program Files\Microsoft
SQL
Server\MSSQL13.MSSQLSERVER\MSSQL\DAT
A\classlog.ldf',
     SIZE = 5MB,
     MAXSIZE = 25MB,
     FILEGROWTH = 5MB ) ;
GO
```

The example will create a database named "Class." Since we have not specified the keyword PRIMARY, then the first file named "classdat" will become the primary file. Since we have not specified the MB or KB in the size of the file, then MB will be used and this will be allocated in Megabytes.

Alter Database

This can be used to modify the database or any files or filegroups associated with the database. You can use it to add or remove files from the database, change the collation of the database, and change the database options. The snapshots for the database cannot be changed. If you need to change the options for the database which are associated with replication, just use the sp-replicationboption.

ALTER DATABASE File and Filegroup Options

This helps in the modification of files and filegroups which are associated with a particular SQL Server database.

It can be used for adding or removing files and filegroups from SQL Server database, as well as for changing the attributes of the database or its files or filegroups. It takes the following syntax:

ALTER DATABASE database_name
{
  <add_or_modify_files>
  | <add_or_modify_filegroups>
}
[;]

<add_or_modify_files>::=
{
  ADD FILE <filespec> [,...n]
    [TO FILEGROUP { filegroup_name }]
  | ADD LOG FILE <filespec> [,...n]
  | REMOVE FILE logical_file_name
  | MODIFY FILE <filespec>
}

<filespec>::=
(
  NAME = logical_file_name
  [, NEWNAME = new_logical_name]
  [, FILENAME = {'os_file_name' | 'filestream_path'
| 'memory_optimized_data_path' }]

  [, SIZE = size [KB | MB | GB | TB]]
  [, MAXSIZE = { max_size [KB | MB | GB | TB] |
UNLIMITED }]

  [, FILEGROWTH = growth_increment [KB | MB |
GB | TB| %]]

  [, OFFLINE]
)

<add_or_modify_filegroups>::=

```
{
  | ADD FILEGROUP filegroup_name
    [ CONTAINS FILESTREAM | CONTAINS
MEMORY_OPTIMIZED_DATA ]

  | REMOVE FILEGROUP filegroup_name
  | MODIFY FILEGROUP filegroup_name
    { <filegroup_updatability_option>
    | DEFAULT
    | NAME = new_filegroup_name
    | { AUTOGROW_SINGLE_FILE |
AUTOGROW_ALL_FILES }
    }
}
<filegroup_updatability_option>::=
{
  { READONLY | READWRITE }
  | { READ_ONLY | READ_WRITE }
}
```

The following are some of the arguments used in the syntax;

1. database_name- this is the name of the database which is to be modified.

2. ADD FILE- this is for adding a file to the database.

3. TO FILEGROUP { FILEGROUP_NAME }- specifies the name of the filegroup into which we will add the specified file.

4. ADD LOG FILE- a log file will be added to the named database.

5. REMOVE FILE LOGICAL_FILE_NAME- *FOR REMOVING THE LOGICAL DESCRIPTION OF A FILE FROM THE SQL SERVER INSTANCE AND DELETING THE PHYSICAL FILE. ONLY AN EMPTY FILE CAN BE REMOVED.*

6. LOGICAL_FILE_NAME- *THIS IS THE LOGICAL NAME TO BE USED IN SQL SERVER WHEN REFERENCING A FILE.*

7. MODIFY FILE- specifies the file which is to be modified. Note that only one <filespec> may be modified at a time. The NAME has to be specified in the <filespec> so as to identify the file which is to be modified. If you need to change the logical name of a log file or data file, its name should be specified by use of the NAME clause as shown below:

MODIFY FILE (NAME = logical_file_name, NEWNAME = new_logical_name)
To move a log file or a data file to some new location, use the NAME clause to specify the current name for the logical file, and then the path and the operating system file name in FILENAME clause. Example:

MODIFY FILE (NAME = logical_file_name, FILENAME = ' new_path/os_file_name ')

If you need to add a file to your database, the following example will guide you:

USE master;
GO
ALTER DATABASE Class
ADD FILE
(
  NAME = TestFile1,

  FILENAME = 'C:\Program Files\Microsoft SQL Server\MSSQL13.MSSQLSERVER\MSSQL\DATA\test dat2.ndf',

  SIZE = 5MB,
  MAXSIZE = 100MB,

```
     FILEGROWTH = 5MB
);
GO
```

Note that the file will grow to a maximum size of 100 MB. If you need to add a filegroup composed of two files to the database, be guided by the following example:

```
USE master
GO
ALTER DATABASE Class
ADD FILEGROUP Test1FG1;
GO
ALTER DATABASE Class
ADD FILE
(
   NAME = test1dat3,

   FILENAME = 'C:\Program Files\Microsoft SQL
Server\MSSQL13.MSSQLSERVER\MSSQL\DATA\t1d
at3.ndf',

   SIZE = 5MB,
   MAXSIZE = 100MB,
   FILEGROWTH = 5MB
),
(
   NAME = test1dat4,
   FILENAME = 'C:\Program Files\Microsoft SQL
Server\MSSQL13.MSSQLSERVER\MSSQL\DATA\t1d
at4.ndf',

   SIZE = 5MB,
   MAXSIZE = 100MB,
   FILEGROWTH = 5MB
)
TO FILEGROUP Test1FG1;
GO
```

The files will have a size of 5 MB. The following example demonstrates how you can add two log files to the Class database. The log files have a size of 5 MB:

```
USE master;
GO
ALTER DATABASE Class
ADD LOG FILE
(
   NAME = test1log2,

   FILENAME = 'C:\Program Files\Microsoft SQL
Server\MSSQL13.MSSQLSERVER\MSSQL\DATA\test
2log.ldf',

   SIZE = 5MB,
   MAXSIZE = 100MB,
   FILEGROWTH = 5MB
),
(
   NAME = test1log3,

   FILENAME = 'C:\Program Files\Microsoft SQL
Server\MSSQL10_50.MSSQLSERVER\MSSQL\DATA
\test3log.ldf',

   SIZE = 5MB,
   MAXSIZE = 100MB,
   FILEGROWTH = 5MB
);
GO
```

To remove a file from the database, we can use the following example:

```
USE master;
GO
ALTER DATABASE Class
REMOVE FILE test1dat4;
```

GO

The file named "test1dat4" will be removed from the database. You can also modify the size of a file. This calls for you to use ALTER DATABASE with MODIFY FILE which will allow the expansion pf the size of the file. To shrink it, use DBCC SHRINKFILE. The following example shows how to expand the file size:

USE master;
GO

ALTER DATABASE Class
MODIFY FILE
(NAME = test1dat3,
SIZE = 200MB);
GO

The new size of the file is 200 MB. The following example shows how the size of the file can be shrunk up to 100MB:

USE Class;
GO

DBCC SHRINKFILE (Class_data, 100);
GO

USE master;
GO

ALTER DATABASE Class
MODIFY FILE
(NAME = test1dat3,
SIZE = 200MB);
GO

You can also change the location of a file as shown in the following example:

USE master;

```
GO
ALTER DATABASE Class
MODIFY FILE
(
   NAME = Test1dat2,
   FILENAME = N'c:\t1dat2.ndf'
);
GO
```

Note that the FILENAME has been used to specify the new location of the file.

Adding Data and Log File to a Database

The addition of data and log files to the database in SQL Server 2017 can be done from the SQL Server Management Studio or through the Transact-SQL. Note that when adding or removing a file from the database, the BACKUP statement should not be running. For you to be able to do this, you must have the ALTER permission on the database.

Using the SQL Server Management Studio

The following steps will help you add data or a log file to the database by use of the SQL Server Management Studio:

1. Establish a connection to the SQL Server Database Engine and then expand the instance.

2. Expand the section for Databases, and then right click on the database you need to add the files to. Click on "Properties."

3. On the new Window, click on "Files" page.

4. To add the transaction log or data file, click on Add.
5. In the grid for Database files, type in a logical name for the file. Ensure that the name for the file is unique; otherwise, you will get an error.

6. Choose the file type which can be either data or log.

7. In the case of a data file, choose the filegroup in which you need to include the file from the available list, or if you need to create some new group, just choose <new filegroup>. Note that the transaction logs cannot be added to filegroups.

8. Specify the initial size for the file. Ensure that you assign an adequate size capable of accommodating the data you need to hold in the file.

9. If you need to specify how your file will grow, move to the Autogrowth column and then click on (...). You can choose from the options given below:

   • If you need your file to grow as you add more data to it, choose the "Enable Autogrowth" option and then choose the next options:

   • If you need to specify your file to grow in increments, choose "In Megabytes" and then specify a value.

   • If you need to specify your file to grow by a percentage of your current file, choose "In Percentage" and then type in the value.

10. If you need to specify the maximum value for the size of your file, choose the options given below:

   • To set the maximum size for the file to grow to, choose "Restricted File Growth (MB)" and then specify a value.

   • If you need to set the file to grow to the maximum it is needed, choose "Unrestricted File Growth."

- If you need to prevent the file from growing, clear the checkbox for "Enable Autogrowth." After that, the file will not be able to grow beyond the value set in "Initial Size (MB) column.

11. Choose the location for your file. Ensure that the specified path exists before you can add the file.

12. Click "OK."

Using Transact-SQL

You can as well use Transact-SQL so as to add data or log files to your database. The following steps describe how this can be accomplished:

1. Establish a connection to the Database Engine.

2. Move to the Standard Bar and then click on "New Query."

3. Paste the code given below in the query window and then click on "Execute":

```
USE master
GO
ALTER DATABASE Class
ADD FILEGROUP Test1FG1;
GO
ALTER DATABASE Class
ADD FILE
(
   NAME = test1dat3,

   FILENAME = 'C:\Program Files\Microsoft SQL
Server\MSSQL10_50.MSSQLSERVER\MSSQL\
DATA\t1dat3.ndf',

   SIZE = 5MB,
   MAXSIZE = 100MB,
   FILEGROWTH = 5MB
),
(
   NAME = test1dat4,

   FILENAME = 'C:\Program Files\Microsoft SQL
```

```
Server\MSSQL10_50.MSSQLSERVER\MSSQL\
DATA\t1dat4.ndf',

   SIZE = 5MB,
   MAXSIZE = 100MB,
   FILEGROWTH = 5MB
)
TO FILEGROUP Test1FG1;
GO
```

The code adds a file group made up of two files to the database. The file group has been named Test1FG1 with two files of 5MB.

Deleting Data and Log Files from the Database

The deletion of data and log files from SQL Server 2017 can be done from the SQL Server Management Studio as well as using the Transact-SQL. Let us discuss how this can be done.

Note that for you to be able to delete a file, it must be empty. You should also have the ALTER database permission on the database.

Using the SQL Server Management Studio

The deletion of data or log files from the database by the use of SQL Server Management Studio can be done as follows:

1. Establish a connection to the instance of SQL Server Database Engine from the Object Explorer and then expand the instance.

2. Expand the Databases, and identify the database with the file to be deleted then right on it. Click on Properties.

3. Choose the Files page.

4. In the grid for "Database files," choose the file which you need to delete and then click on "Remove."

5. Click "OK."

Using Transact-SQL

This can be used for deletion of data or log file by following the steps given below:

1. Establish a connection to the Database Engine.

2. Navigate to the Standard Bar and then click on New Query.

3. Paste the following code into the window:

    ```
    USE master;
    GO
    ALTER DATABASE Class
    REMOVE FILE test1dat4;
    GO
    ```

The script given above will remove the file named test1dat4.

Increasing database Size

The size of a database in SQL Server 2017 can be increased. This can be done from the SQL Server Management Studio or by use of the Transact-SQL. To increase the database size, we expand the existing data or the log file or add a new file to the database.

Note that it is impossible for you to add or remove a file as the Backup statement is already running. You should also have the ALTER permission on the database.

Using the SQL Server Management Studio

The size of the database can be increased as follows:

1. Establish a connection to the instance of Database Instance and then expand the database instance.

2. Expand the Databases section, identify the database whose size is to be increased, right click it, and then choose Properties.

3. From the Database Properties window, click on the Files page.
4. If you need to increase the size of an existing file, just move to the "Initial Size (MB)" column of the file and then type in a larger value. Note that the size of the database should be increased by not less than 1 MB.

5. If you increase the database size by creating a new file, just click on Add and then specify the details for the new file.

6. Click OK so as to complete.

Using Transact-SQL

The size of the database can be increased as follows:

1. Establish a connection to the Database Engine.

2. Move to the Standard bar and then click on New Query.

3. Paste the following code into the window and then click on Execute:

```
USE master;
GO
ALTER DATABASE Class
MODIFY FILE
   (NAME = test1dat3,
   SIZE = 20MB);
GO
```

In the above example, we are increasing the size of the file named test1dat3.

Chapter 4- Creating User-Defined Data Type Alias

The creation of a user-defined alias in SQL Server 2017 can be done either from the SQL Server Management Studio or by use of the Transact-SQL. Note that the name that you choose to use for the alias must meet the rules and regulations for defining identifiers. For you to be able the alias, you must have the CREATE TYPE permission on the database as well as the ALTER permission on the scheme name.

If you don't specify the schema name, the default name resolution rules for determination of the schema for current user will apply.

Using SQL Server Management Studio

If you need to create some user-defined types in SQL Server from the Management Studio, follow the steps given below:

1. Expand the Databases in the Object Explorer, expand the database you need, expand Programmability, expand Types, right click the User-Defined Data Types, and then click on "New User-Defined Data Type."

Allow Nulls

You should also specify whether the User-Defined type will be able to accept NULL values or not.

Data Type

Choose a base data type from the provided list box. This will have the data types other than geometry, geography, sysname, hierarchyid, xml and timestamp data types.

Default

You can choose a rule or a default which will be bound to the user-defined data alias.

Name

If you need to create a new user-defined data type alias, then you have to give it a unique name which will be used across the database to identify it. The characters must match the sysname data type.

Scale

This defines the maximum decimal digits which can be on the right of decimal digit.

You should also choose a schema and the maximum storage size for the user-defined data type alias.

2. In the dialog box for "New User-defined Data Type" and in Schema box, enter the schema which will hold the data type alias, or make use of browse button so as to browse for the schema.
3. Type the alias name in the Name box.

4. Choose the data type of the alias from the "Data type" box.

5. Fill the boxes for Length, Precision, and Scale for the data type. If you need it to allow nulls, check the box for "Allow Nulls."

6. In the Binding area, complete the Default or Rule boxes if you need to bind a default or rule to your new data type alias.

Using Transact-SQL

A user-defined data type alias can be created as follows:

1. Establish a connection to the Database Engine.

2. Click "New Query" from the Standard bar.

3. Paste the code given below to the window then click on "Execute":

   CREATE TYPE ssn
   FROM varchar(11) NOT NULL ;

Chapter 5 – Creating a Full Database Backup

There are three ways that you can create a full database backup in SQL Server 2017. These include by use of SQL Server Management Studio, by use of Transact-SQL, and by use of PowerShell.

It is good for you to note that the BACKUP statement cannot be used in an implicit or explicit transaction. If you create a database backup of a recent SQL Server version, then it is impossible for you to restore a later version of the same.

Using SQL Server Management Studio

Once you have used the SQL Server Management Studio to create a backup, you can get the corresponding Transact-SQL script by clicking on the "Script" button. You will then be asked to select the destination for the script. The backup can be created as follows:

1. Establish a connection to the right Database Engine and then click on the server name so as to expand the server tree.

2. Expand the Databases section and choose a user database or expand the "System Databases" section and then choose a system database.

3. Right click the database; choose Tasks, and then "Back Up." You will be presented with the dialog box for "Back Up Database."
4. Verify the name of the database from the Database drop down list. You can also choose a different database if you need.

5. The text box for "Recovery Model" is only for reference. This can be FULL, BULK_LOGGED, or SIMPLE and you can perform a backup for all of these.

6. In the drop-down list for "Backup type," choose "Full." Note that a differential backup can be done after a full database backup.

7. You can also check the "Copy-only backup" checkbox so as to create a copy-only backup. This will be different from the conventional SQL Server backups.

8. Select the radio button for Database for a Backup component.

9. In the section for Destination, use the drop-down for "Back up to" so as to choose the backup destination. If you need to add some other backup destinations or objects, click on "Add."

    If you need to remove a backup destination, choose it, and then click on "Remove." To see what is contained in a particular backup destination, just choose it and then click on "Contents."

10. If you need to view or choose media options, click on "Media Options" in the pane for "Select a page."

11. Click on any of the following so as to choose an "Overwrite Media" option:

    Back up to the existing media set:

    In the case of this option, you can click "Append to the existing backup set" or "Overwrite all existing backup sets." If you need the backup operation to verify date and time for the expiration of the media set and backup, choose "Check media sct name and backup set expiration."

    Back up to a new media set, and erase all existing backup sets

For this, just provide a name in the text box for "New media set name." You can then describe this media set in the text for "New media set description."

12. In the section for "reliability." check the following, but this is optional:

    - Verify the backup once it is finished.

    - Perform a checksum before writing to the media.

    - Continue on error.

13. The section for "Transaction log" will be inactive unless you are backing up a transaction log.

14. To view or choose backup options, click on "Backup Options" from the "Select a page" pane.

15. In the text box for "Name," feel free to specify a different name for the backup set. In the text box for "Description," you can type a description for the backup set.

16. Specify the expiration date for the backup set.

17. In the section for "Compression," choose the compression level for the backup.

18. You may also need to encrypt the backup. If this is the case, use the "Encrypt backup" option located in the "Encryption" section. The "Algorithm" section will allow you to choose the algorithm to be used for encryption. If you need to choose an existing asymmetric key or certificate, use the drop down list for "Certificate or Asymmetric key."

Full back up to disk to the default location

We want to back up our Class database at the disk at the default backup location.

1. Establish a connection to the Database Engine and then expand the instance.

2. Expand the Databases section, right click on Class database, point to Tasks, and then choose "Back Up..."

3. Click "OK."

Full back up to disk to the non-default location

In this example, we need to back up our Class database to "F:\MSSQL\BAK." Here are the steps:

1. Establish a connection to the Database Engine and then expand the instance.

2. Expand the Databases section, right click on Class database, point to Tasks, and then choose "Back Up..."

3. In the Destination section of General page, choose 'Disk" from the drop-down list for "Back up to:"

4. Click on "Remove" for all the backup files in existence to be removed.

5. Click on "Add," and the dialog box for "Select Backup Destination" will be opened.

6. In the text box for "file name," type "F:\MSSQL\BAK\Class_20170601.bak."

7. Click OK and OK in the next window.

Creation of an Encrypted Backup

We now need to back up our Class database with encryption. The backup will be saved in the default location. We have created the database master key and the certificate.

1. Establish a connection to the Database Engine and then expand the instance.

2. Expand the Databases section, right click on Class database, point to Tasks, and then choose "Back Up..."

3. In the Destination section of General page, choose 'Disk" from the drop-down list for "Back up to:"

4. On the page for "Media Options" and in "Overwrite media" section, choose "Back up to a new media set, and erase all existing backup sets."

5. On the page for "Backup Options" and in "Encryption" section, select the checkbox for "Encrypt backup."

6. In the drop down list for Algorithm, choose "AES 256" as the encryption algorithm.

7. Select the certificate from the "Certificate or Asymmetric key" drop down list.

8. Click OK so as to complete.

Using Transact-SQL

A full database backup can be created as follows:

1. You should run the BACKUP DATABASE statement so as to perform a full database backup while specifying the following parameters:

   The database name, that is, the database to back up.

   The device in which the backup is to be written.

   The Transact-SQL syntax which can be used for a full database backup is as follows:

**BACKUP DATABASE DATABASE
TO BACKUP_DEVICE [,...N]
[WITH WITH_OPTIONS [,...O]] ;**

In this case, "database" is the name of the database to back up. The "BACKUP_DEVICE [,...N]" represents the devices on which the backup is to be done, and it is a list ranging between 1 and 64. The "WITH WITH_OPTIONS [,...O]" helps us specify the options for the backup. Examples of such options include the {COMPRESSION | NO_COMPRESSION} which helps us specify whether a compression will be done on the backup or not and the ENCRYPTION (ALGORITHM, SERVER CERTIFICATE |ASYMMETRIC KEY) which specifies the encryption algorithm to be used.

Backing up to Disk Device

In the following example, we will back up the Class2017 database to the disk, and we will use FORMAT so as to create a new media set:

**USE Class2017;
GO
BACKUP DATABASE Class2017
TO DISK = 'Z:\SQLServerBackups\Class2017.Bak'
  WITH FORMAT,
    MEDIANAME = 'Z_SQLServerBackups',
    NAME = 'Full Backup of Class2017';
GO**

That is it!

Backing Up to Tape

In the following example, we will back up the Class2017 database to a tape and append it to the earlier backups:

USE Class2017;

```
GO
BACKUP DATABASE Class2017
  TO TAPE = '\\.\Tape0'
  WITH NOINIT,
    NAME = 'Full Backup of Class2017';
GO
```

Backing Up to Logical Tape Device

In this example, we will create a logical backup device for a tape drive. The Class2017 database will then be backed up to that device:

-- Create a logical backup device,

-- AdventureWorks2012_Bak_Tape, for tape device \\.\tape0.

```
USE master;
GO
```

```
EXEC sp_addumpdevice 'tape',
'Class2017_Bak_Tape', '\\.\tape0'; USE Class2017;
```

```
GO
BACKUP DATABASE Class2017
  TO Class2017_Bak_Tape
  WITH FORMAT,
    MEDIANAME = ' Class2017_Bak_Tape',
    MEDIADESCRIPTION = '\\.\tape0',
    NAME = 'Full Backup of Class2017';
GO
```

Backup using PowerShell

This can be done by use of the Backup-SqlDatabase cmdlet. If you need to state that this is a full database backup, you have to use the −BackupAction parameter with"Database" which is its default value.

Full Local Backup

In the following example, we will be creating a full database backup of the database named "Class" to the default backup location of server instance which is "Computer\Instance." Here is the example:

Backup-SqlDatabase -ServerInstance Computer\Instance -Database Class -BackupAction Database

Full Database Backup to the Microsoft Azure

In the following example, we will be carrying out a full backup of the Class database located in MyServer instance and the backup will be done to Microsoft Azure Blob Storage service. We have created some stored access policy with write, read, and list rights. We have used the BackupFile parameter so as to specify the location or the URL and the file name for the backup:

import-module sqlps;

$container = 'https://mystorageaccount.blob.core.windows.net/classcontainer';

$FileName = 'Class.bak';
$database = 'Class';
$BackupFile = $container + '/' + $FileName ;

Backup-SqlDatabase -ServerInstance "MyServer" – Database $database -BackupFile $BackupFilc;

Chapter 6- Restoring a Database

In this topic, we will show you how to perform a full database restore by the use of the SQL Server Management Studio.

For you to be able to restore an encrypted database, you should have access to the asymmetric key or the certificate which was used. Without these, you will not be able to restore the database. In case you restore a database from a previous SQL Server version, then it will be automatically upgraded to SQL Server 2017.

The following steps will help you perform a restore of a full backup of a database:

1. Establish a connection to the Database Engine from the Object Explorer.

2. Right click on "Databases" and then choose "Restore Database..."

3. From "General" page, use the section for "Source" so as to specify the source and location of your backup set, and then choose any of the following:

- Database- the database to be restored should be available in the drop-down list, so choose it.

- Device- click on Browse (...) button so as to open the dialog box for "Select backup devices." Choose the media type from the "Backup media device" drop-down list. The Tape option will only be shown if you had mounted it to the computer.

- Add- the kind of dialog box opened after clicking on this will depend on the kind of media you selected.

- Remove- this will remove one or more tapes, files, or logical backup devices.

- Contents- show the media contents for the selected file, logical backup device, or tape.

- Backup media- this will list the media which is selected.

4. In the section for Destination, you will see it populated with the name of the database which has to be populated. If you need to change the database name, just type a new name in the Database text box.

5. In the box for "Restore to," just leave it with the default values. You can click the "Timeline" so as to choose the time at which the recovery will stop.

6. In the grid for "Backup sets to restore," choose the backups which you need to restore.

7. If you need to access the Files dialog box, click on Files from the "Select a page" section.

8. If you need to choose advanced options, you will be able to do it from the Options page of "Restore options" section. Specify any options which you need to use when recovering the database and then click OK.

Conclusion

We have come to the end of this book. SQL Server 2017 is a powerful database management system which can be used in a production environment. The easiest way for you to use SQL Server is through SQL Server Management Studio, which provides you with a graphical user interface. This makes it easy for you to use the SQL Server. The SQL Server Management Studio can be used for performing nearly all the tasks which are performed on the SQL Server. Alternatively, you can use the Transact-SQL to perform the tasks on the SQL Server. This requires you to write scripts and then run them. This is the best way to use SQL Server for those who are experienced or for those with good programming skills. You can write Transact-SQL scripts which can do nearly everything which is done on SQL Server. Note that after backing up a database running on an older version of SQL Server, you can restore it to SQL Server 2017 and it will be automatically upgraded. However, the vice versa is not true, that you cannot backup a SQL Server 2017 database to an older version of SQL Server.